ISRAEL

WITH LOVE

ISRAEL

WITH LOVE

Paintings and text by

DOROTHY RICE

GLEN HOUSE COMMUNICATIONS

Contents

Pages 2-3

The Temple Mount Southern Wall

Three great religions, Judaism, Christianity, and Islam, hold the Temple Mount in great reverence. For Jews, it is a most sacred sanctuary, where the two Great Temples once stood. For Christians, it marks the site of Jesus' triumphal return after the Resurrection. For Muslims, it is the place from which Mohammed ascended to Heaven. Constructed on the ruins of a Byzantine church is the magnificent Al-Aksa Mosque, which sits atop the remnants of Solomon's Stables, immense subterranean chambers where horses and chariots were housed when Crusaders used the Temple Mount as their headquarters. In 1951, Jordan's King Abdullah was assassinated here in front of his grandson, King Hussein of Jordan, by a fanatical Muslim. And in 1977, President Anwar Sadat of Egypt prayed here.

Pages 6-7

Akko harbor view.

Library of Congress Cataloging-in-Publication Data:
Rice, Dorothy.
    Israel with love/paintings and text by Dorothy Rice.—1st ed.
            p.   cm.
    Includes index.
    Summary: Watercolor paintings depict the beauty and mystery of Israel.
    ISBN 0-918269-01-6
    1. Israel--Description and travel—1991.
2. Israel in art. 3. Rice, Dorothy. [1. Israel—Description and travel. 2. Israel in art.] I. Title.
DS107.5R53 1992
759/13--dc20   92-10106
                        CIP
                        AC

Printed and bound by Dai Nippon, Tokyo, Japan

Published by
GLEN HOUSE COMMUNICATIONS
P.O. Box 3663
Beverly Hills, California 90212-0666.

4

Rice

Dead Sea Scrolls

Hidden in the Judean wilderness for two thousand years, these recently discovered scrolls were found in the region where, according to the Old Testament, a wrathful Lord rained fire and brimstone upon Sodom and Gomorrah. Inscripted in ancient Hebrew, the scrolls provide a glimpse into the development of Judaism and Christianity. Representing one of the most important historical, archaeological, and religious discoveries of the ages, the original scrolls are on display in the beautiful Chamber of the Book of the Shrine at the Israel Museum in Jerusalem.

Dedicated to the memory of

Sarah and Hyman Cohen

and

Pearl and Harry Ribak

Special thanks to

Norma and Milton L. Cohen

for making this book possible

The Great Hurva Synagogue and Minaret

Seeming to defy gravity, this solitary archway is all that remains of the original Great Hurva, meaning *ruin*. Burned down in 1720 and rebuilt, it was destroyed again during the War of Independence. Located below the Hurva is the Ramban Synagogue, still used for daily prayer.

Acknowledgments

My thanks to:

Stanley Chase for his dedication and invaluable work in making this book a reality;

The Israel Histadrut Foundation for their cooperation and support from the beginning of the project to its publication; President Herbert Rothman and Executive Vice President Alvin Smolin;

Abe Frank for his constant moral support;

Eytan Bentsur, who convinced me to do this book;

President Chaim Herzog of Israel and Mayor Teddy Kollek of Jerusalem for generously giving their time to pose for me;

Eliyahu Honig, assistant Vice President of the Hebrew University, whose knowledge of Israel was very helpful;

The Jerusalem Foundation, who invited me to Israel; Michael Jay Solomon, Neal Levy, Ruth Cheshin, and Csynthia Savage;

Dana Levy and D.J. Choi for the book and jacket design;

Editorial Consultants Mallory Tarcher, Fred Perry, Lynette Padwa, Bruce Boettcher, Ruth Green-Conn, Helaina Indictor, Ahuva Rabani, Dianne Woo, and Kevin Corcoran;

Yitzchak Dekel, Michael Dougherty, Arie Sommer, David and Margalit Friedman, Tammy and Michael Abramowitz, Berta and Yehuda Handel, Sheila and Fritz Glazer, Ahuva and Yifrach Gavish, and Zehava Yanouka for their help along the way.

In memory of my father, Alexander Rice, whose exceptional talent as an artist inspired me.

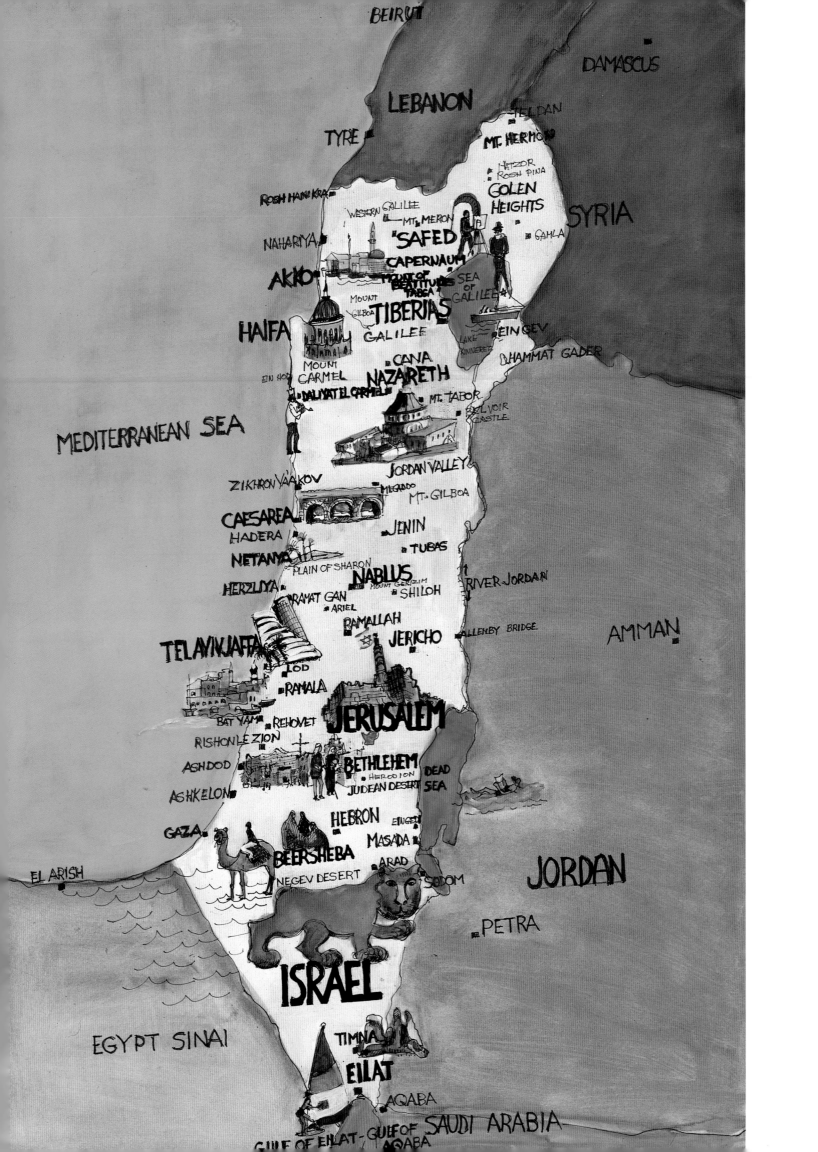

Israel:

What Is It?

MUCH HAS BEEN WRITTEN ABOUT ISRAEL. BUT NOTH-
ing I have read quite prepared me for the
experience until I went to Israel myself. My
journey was one of discovery and learning. I was
struck by the great beauty and mystery of this ancient land—and the
remarkable progress made by its people.

I remember the blue-and-white Israeli flags fluttering everywhere. The hordes of happy children. The new pioneers walking the
streets, the colors of many nations reflected in their faces. The vibrant hues
and abundance of flowers and trees. The marvelous historical sites and
excavations. The mystery of the varied religious peoples. The clean, clear
air of Jerusalem and its buildings of local golden stone. The breeze and
warm sunlight of Caesarea. The hills of Haifa reaching down to the
harbor. The medieval cobblestoned alleys of mystic Safed, its old synagogues, and the artists who paint their visions of the Cabala. The balmy
days of Tiberias along the bluest water of the Sea of Galilee, its serious,
handsome children eating ice cream at the end of the day on the
promenade at the edge of the water. The young couples all over Israel
getting married in elaborate rented wedding gowns and tuxedos, photog-
raphers chasing them down the street. The trip through the Negev
Desert, riding past the Bedouin tents with their television antennas. The
panoramic view of the Dead Sea from the top of the ancient fortress of
Masada. The bitter smell of sulphur and salt as I floated on the Dead Sea.

What a feeling to walk the biblical streets and countryside that
seem to have existed since the beginning of time. What an inspiration.
What a challenge. What a joy.

Israel, the perfect weather, the perfect light in which to paint.
How happy I was to come!

I hope you enjoy the journey through these pages as much as I
enjoyed mine.

With love,

Dorothy Rice

ISRAEL

A CHRONOLOGY

NEW STONE AGE
NEOLITHIC: 8000–4500 BC

8000 BC—Jericho, a walled city. Agriculture. Domestic animals.

COPPER–STONE AGE
CHALCOLITHIC: 4500–3100 BC

EARLY BRONZE AGE:
3100–2200 BC

MIDDLE BRONZE AGE:
2200–1550 BC

2000 BC—Canaanite settlement.

1926 BC—Arrival of Abraham in Canaan.

1700–1550 BC—Patriarch period. Hyksos conquers Egypt and Canaan.

1630 BC—Jacob's family migrates to Egypt.

LATE BRONZE AGE: 1550–1020 BC

1550–1200 BC—Egypt expels Hyksos and dominates Canaan.

1300–1250 BC—Moses leads exodus from Egypt.

1250 BC—Joshua's conquest.

IRON AGE: 1200–586 BC

1200 BC—Philistines invade Canaan.

UNITED KINGDOM: 1020–538 BC

1020–1004 BC—Saul, first King of Israel.

1004 BC—Defeat of the Philistines. David unites Kingdom.

Greeter at the Western Wall

965–932 BC—Solomon builds Jerusalem's First Temple.

932–722 BC—Divided Kingdom: Israel (north), Judah (south).

735–722 BC—Assyrians conquer north. Dispersion of ten tribes.

587–539 BC—Babylonians destroy Judah, Jerusalem, and Temple.

PERSIAN ERA: 538–333 BC

520 BC—Jews return from Babylonian exile. Second Temple. Spiritual revival.

HELLENISTIC ERA: 333–63 BC

333 BC—Alexander the Great conquers the area.

167–143 BC—Maccabean revolt.

143–63 BC—Hasmonean dynasty.

ROMAN ERA: 63 BC–AD 326

63 BC—Pompey conquers Jerusalem for Rome.

63–4 BC—Herod the Great.

4 BC-AD 39—Herod Antipater.

AD 33—Crucifixion of Jesus.

David's Citadel

Roman aqueduct near Cæsarea

66–70—Jews revolt against Rome. Second Temple destroyed.

73—Masada falls.

132–135—Bar-Kochba revolt.

250–303—Decius and Diocletian persecute Christians.

BYZANTINE ERA: 326–638

326—Constantine builds great churches.

527—Justinian is Emperor.

EARLY ARAB ERA: 638–1098

622—Mohammed's hejira. Islam begins.

638—Muslim conquest of Jerusalem.

661–750—Omayyad Caliphate. Seat in Damascus.

CRUSADER ERA: 1099–1187

1099—First Crusade. Latin Kingdom of Jerusalem established.

1187—Saladin defeats Crusaders at Hattin.

1192—Crusader Kingdom based at Akko.

1291—Crusaders driven from land by Mamelukes.

MAMELUKE ERA: 1260–1517

1260—Egypt's Mamelukes conquer Jerusalem and rule for 250 years.

OTTOMAN ERA: 1517–1917

1517—Ottoman Turks conquer Palestine.

1543—Sultan Suleiman rebuilds Jerusalem's walls.

1799— Napoleon campaigns from Egypt to Akko.

1882—Jews start coming from Eastern Europe.

1897—Theodore Herzl. First Zionist Congress in Basle, Switzerland.

1909—Tel Aviv founded. First Kibbutz founded on Lake Kinneret.

1917—Balfour Declaration.

BRITISH ERA: 1917–1948

1917–1918—British drive Turks out.

1922–1948—British Mandate over Palestine.

MODERN ISRAEL ERA: 1948–PRESENT

May 14, 1948—Jews declare State. David Ben Gurion becomes first Prime Minister. Arab armies invade.

1956—Sinai Campaign.

1967—Six Day War.

1973—October Yom Kippur War.

1979—Peace treaty (Israel and Egypt).

1981—Israeli jets destroy Iraqi nuclear reactor.

1982–1985—Lebanon War.

1983—Chaim Herzog becomes President of Israel.

February 1991—Gulf War. Iraqi scud missiles hit Israel.

Fall 1991—Israeli–Arab peace conference begins in Madrid.

President Chaim Herzog

Church of the Nativity in Bethlehem

Jerusalem

*J*ERUSALEM, THE CITY THAT CONTAINS THE HOLIEST shrines of three religions—Judaism, Christianity, and Islam—has been praised and sung about through the ages. For over three thousand years combatants have come from afar, seeking to possess a piece of it or conquer it all. It has been conquered and reconquered by Canaanites, Israelites, Assyrians, Babylonians, Greeks, Romans, Jews, Muslims, and Crusaders. Centuries of worshipers and pilgrims have made their way to it from all parts of the world. Nothing quite prepared me for my first sight of Jerusalem. Nothing read or seen can quite define its mysticism. Its beauty and mystique are so powerful that they overwhelm you. Chants and the sound of bells are in the air. The flowers and trees in bloom envelop its old walls and streets. Known also as Jerusalem the Golden, the city is surrounded by golden hills that shimmer in the everlasting sunlight. The Old City gleams in varying shades of gold and purple, orange and blue from morning to dusk. At night it is lit by its many lights and the moon and stars, as if the heavens have reached down to embrace it with love. Jerusalem is a city where old thrives next to new, where Orthodox religious Jews walk next to nuns in their long habits and Arabs in keffiye headdress. It is a city that preserves a remnant from each of its conquering foes, and at the same time gladly assimilates new people and modern ways.

Mount Scopus

Poised majestically on Mount Scopus, the ancient "Hill of the Watchman," Hebrew University draws both the eye and the heart. The University's founders were all men of vision: Albert Einstein, Sigmund Freud, Martin Buber, and Chaim Weizmann, who inaugurated the University in 1925 and later became Israel's first President. The road to the University leads from the past to the future, blending high technology with a love for the humanities, arts, and sciences.

Jerusalem

City of David and capital of Israel

A CHRONOLOGY

BIBLICAL ERA: 1004–586 BC

1004 BC—King David captures Jerusalem and makes it the capital of the United Kingdom of Israel.

961–922 BC— King Solomon builds the First Temple on the site chosen by his father, King David.

931 BC—Solomon's kingdom is split into Judah and Israel.

701 BC—Assyrian King Sennacherib tries in vain to seize Jerusalem.

FIRST DIASPORA

587 BC—Nebuchadnezzar, King of Babylon, destroys Jerusalem and its Temple and exiles the Jews to Babylon.

PERSIAN ERA: 538–333 BC

538–537 BC—Cyrus, King of Persia, issues historic edict of the repatriation of the exiles. The Jews return from Babylon.

520–516 BC—The Second Temple is rebuilt.

444 BC—City wall built by Nehemiah.

Via Dolorosa

Damascus Gate

HELLENISTIC ERA: 333–63 BC

333 BC—Alexander the Great of Macedonia captures Palestine.

313 BC—Ptolemy I, Alexander's general, seizes Jerusalem and launches the Ptolemian dynasty of Egypt.

167–164 BC—Antiochus IV Epiphanes desecrates the Temple. Judah Maccabee liberates Jerusalem from Greek domination.

ROMAN ERA: 63 BC–AD 326

63 BC—Pompey enters Jerusalem.

37 BC—Pompey appoints Herod King to succeed Antigonus, the last of the Hasmoneans to rule.

20 BC—King Herod rebuilds Jerusalem and its Temple.

AD 33—Jesus of Nazareth is crucified by order of Pontius Pilate.

66–70—War of the Jews ends in the fall of Jerusalem and the destruction of the Second Temple.

132–153—Short-lived liberation of Jerusalem after Bar-Kochba's revolt ends with the crushing of the revolt by Hadrian. Jerusalem is razed, then renamed Aelia Capitolina. Jews are expelled.

BYZANTINE ERA: 326–638

326–333—Byzantine Emperor Constantine and his mother, Queen Helena, arrive in Jerusalem to launch an age of building.

614–629—Short-lived Persian conquest of Jerusalem with Jewish aid. Emperor Heraclius restores Jerusalem to Byzantine fold.

632—Death of Mohammed.

ARAB ERA: 638–1099

638—Caliph Omar overruns Jerusalem.

692—Caliph Abd Al-Malik builds the Dome of the Rock.

1010—Caliph El Hakim orders the destruction of synagogues and churches.

Mea Shearim

CRUSADER ERA: 1099–1187

1099—Godfrey liberates Jerusalem during the first Crusade.

1187—Saladin ousts the Crusaders, but allows the Jews to return.

1192—Richard the Lionheart fails to conquer Jerusalem.

1244—Jerusalem is sacked by the Turks. Crusader rule ends.

MAMELUKE ERA: 1260–1517

1260—Egypt's Mamelukes capture Jerusalem and rule for 250 years.

OTTOMAN ERA: 1517–1917

1517—Mamelukes destroyed by Turks. Sultan Selim I launches a 400-year Ottoman control of Jerusalem.

1535—Suleiman the Magnificent rebuilds the city walls. In 1541 the Muslims seal the Golden Gate to prevent the Jewish Messiah from entering the city.

1838—First British consulate opens in Jerusalem.

1859–1869—Mishkenot Sha'ananim, first Jewish settlement, is built outside Old City walls.

1898—Herzl meets with Kaiser Wilhelm II.

BRITISH ERA: 1917–1948

1917—General Allenby conquers Jerusalem. British mandatory rule begins in 1922.

1925—Lord Balfour and Chaim Weizmann inaugurate Hebrew University on Mount Scopus. Albert Einstein delivers first lecture.

1938—Hadassah University Hospital reopened on Mount Scopus.

May 14, 1948—Creation of the State of Israel.

1948–1949—The War of Independence. Jerusalem is divided. Defying a United Nations resolution, the Arab Legion captures the Old City and destroys 58 synagogues, expelling the Jewish population.

MODERN ERA: 1949–PRESENT

1956—Sinai Campaign.

1961–62—Eichmann trial.

1964—Visit of Pope Paul VI.

1965—Teddy Kollek becomes Mayor of Jerusalem

1966—New Knesset building inaugurated.

1967—The Six Day War. Jerusalem reunited under Israeli sovereignty.

1973—Yom Kippur War.

1977—President Sadat addresses the Knesset, launching peace with Egypt.

1980—A special law by the Knesset confirms East and West Jerusalem united as the capital of Israel.

1990—The U.S. Congress resolves that Jerusalem should remain Israel's capital.

Mayor Teddy Kollek

Bus stop in East Jerusalem

Across from the Damascus Gate where Arabs catch the bus to Arab towns on the West Bank.

The Damascus Gate

Marking the end of the road from Damascus, this impressive structure was built by Suleiman the Magnificent in the 16th century. Anchored to the foundations laid during the time of Herod, the massive entrance is the most beautifully decorated gate in the city.

next page >

Jesus' garden tomb

Serenity permeates this quiet locale in East Jerusalem, believed by Protestants to be the true place where Jesus was entombed. Maintained by the Anglican Church, these ancient pathways and beautiful English gardens are visited by Christian faithful from all over the world. While I was painting here, I noticed people from many different countries forming small prayer groups throughout the garden.

< Montefiore Windmill

View from my window

Opposite the Old City between the Jaffa Gate and Mount Zion, the first neighborhood to be established outside the Jewish Quarter of the Old City of Jerusalem was Mishkenot Sha'ananim, which means *Dwelling of Tranquility.* It was built by the British-Jewish philanthropist Sir Moses Montefiore in 1860, with funds provided by American philanthropist Judah Touro of New Orleans. Abandoned in 1948 by its Jewish inhabitants because of its proximity to the invading Jordanian forces, it was liberated in the Six Day War in 1967. It also houses an art gallery and the Jerusalem Music Center. The Jerusalem Foundation restored the entire area of the Yemin Moshe Quarter, renovating the old buildings of Mishkenot Sha'ananim. Many of the great musicians of the world have stayed here, such as Pablo Casals, Zubin Mehta, Yehudi Menuhin, Arthur Rubinstein, and Isaac Stern; artists such as Alexander Calder, Marc Chagall, and Robert Rauschenberg: writers such as Graham Greene, Jean-Paul Sartre, Simone de Beauvoir, Saul Bellow, Friedrich Dürrenmatt, Alan Silitoe, Irving Stone, Leon Uris, and Herman Wouk.

I woke up to the breathtaking sight of the wall of the Old City of Jerusalem; the sun created a dazzling display of such beauty that it prompted me to immediately take out my brushes and begin to paint. I was fortunate to be invited by the Jerusalem Foundation to stay at the Mishkenot Sha'ananim, where I had the Arthur Rubinstein suite. My first days were spent exploring the city. At night the colors deepened to violet and golden hues that were so compelling it was hard to close the curtains to sleep. It inspired me to start my painting journey through Jerusalem. Each morning I carried my art supplies and easel down the many stone steps of the Mishkenot Sha'ananim and along a dirt road and through the Khutzot HaYotzer, the arts and crafts compound with its many shops and studios of Israeli artisans, and then across the road to the Jaffa Gate to enter the Old City.

Inside the Jaffa Gate

The Arab shopkeepers in the souk
surrounded me as I painted inside
the Jaffa Gate, making suggestions
and finally approving my work.
They said, "The painting is true, it
is painted as it is."

< top

Jaffa Gate

Considered to be the most popular
entrance into the Old City, the
Jaffa Gate and the formidable walls
surrounding the city were built in
1538 by Suleiman the Magnificent, who was so angered when his
architects failed to include Mount
Zion within the walls that he had
the men promptly executed.

< bottom

Walking to the Jaffa Gate

Clergy coming out of the Souk

King David's Citadel

Built in 40 BC by Herod the Great, this Citadel was a virtual fortress with two massive palaces, vast gardens, and three huge towers which Herod named after his brother Phasael, his friend Hippius, and his wife Mariamme—whom Herod later murdered. Phasael's tower and the foundation are all that remain of the original structure.

Entering King David's Citadel

Through the Jaffa Gate and to the right is King David's Citadel, also called the Tower of David. Across the moat at the entrance to the Citadel you may begin a fabulous visit to the Museum of the History of Jerusalem.

The Souk

Inside the Jaffa Gate at the far end of the square is the entrance to the souk, or shuk—the Arab bazaar. You enter a narrow passageway down many stone steps worn to a smooth sheen after centuries of use. Almost within reach of out-stretched arms are the small colorful shops of the Arab shop-keepers and Druze merchants. The shouts of shopkeepers and the smell of incense and exotic food in the air heightens the sense of mystery and danger. It was easy to get lost within this labyrinth of alleyways as I passed the Mameluke architecture, the many churches, cathedrals, monasteries, mosques, hospices, and courtyards to find my way to the Church of the Holy Sepulchre.

View from King David's Citadel

There are panoramic views of the city from every part of the ram-parts of the Citadel. The Citadel also presents brilliant light and sound shows in the evening, as well as dramatic displays of Jerusa-lem through the ages and films explaining the city's history.

*En route to the Church of
the Holy Sepulchre*

CHURCH OF THE HOLY SEPULCHRE

I visited the Church of the Holy
Sepulchre three times. After doing a
painting of the courtyard, I entered
the church for the first time and
went to the Greek Orthodox shrine.
In the semidarkness I felt a special
poignancy filled with mystique that
compelled me to paint inside the
church. On my second visit I was
surrounded by an interested audi-
ence of nuns and clergy who
watched my progress. I was in-
trigued by the faces around me. My
favorite face was that of the Coptic
priest. I came back a third time to
do his portrait. The Church of the

Holy Sepulchre is the most holy site
in Christianity, marking the site of
the crucifixion, burial, and resurrection of Jesus. Destruction and
rivalries between various church
factions have marred the sanctity of
this site for centuries. Built by
Emperor Constantine in the 4th
century after his mother, Helena,
identified the location as Christ's
tomb, the church was later destroyed
by invading Persians. Rebuilt by
Modestus, a Byzantine abbot, it
stood until it was again toppled by
the mad Caliph El Hakim, who
rampaged through Christendom

intent on destroying all churches.
Ironically, he repented two years later
and ordered its reconstruction. The
present church was built by Crusaders
in the 12th century. Burned to the
ground in 1808, the building remains
unfinished today and was still under
construction during my visit. Due to
centuries of infighting for possession
of various shrines within the Holy
Sepulchre, the Turks finally inter-
ceded in 1852, passing a decree
which partitioned the church to all six
Christian factions: the Copt; the
Latin; the Greek, Armenian, and
Syrian Orthodox; and the Ethiopian.

Inside the Church of the Holy Sepulchre

In the great Rotunda to the right, the tomb of Christ is enclosed in a 19th-century aedicule. This tiny chamber is only large enough for a few people to enter at one time. Inside the aedicule a Greek priest was praying amidst flowers and incense.

Clergy in the Church

Coptic Priest >

The serene face of this Coptic priest belies a century and a half of conflict between his own Egyptian Christian sect and the Ethiopian Christians. Both groups maintain nearby monasteries. The altar in the Chapel of the Copts, located in the Church of the Holy Sepulchre, rests atop a portion of the rock from the traditional tomb of Christ.

Lion's Gate

Flanked by four lions, the formidable 16th-century structure is called Stephen's Gate by Christians, who believe that Stephen the Martyr was stoned to death here. Built by Suleiman the Magnificent, this was the entrance used by Israeli forces when they penetrated the Old City during the Six Day War. Located in the Arab Quarter, the gate leads to the Via Dolorosa, where you can sample the local cuisine.

Crusader fruit market, Arab Quarter

Light enters the bazaar through the square opening at the top of the vaults. This multilingual food market is very popular among the different peoples of Jerusalem. It was delightful to smell the spices and herbs that permeated the whole area.

< Armenian Convent St. Jaques

Prayerful song from the nunnery fills the air in this tranquil section of the Armenian Quarter. Located on the way from the Citadel to Zion Gate and Mount Zion are the Armenian Museum and the St. James Cathedral, a stunningly beautiful church containing the throne of St. James the Lesser. Each year, on the day of the feast of St. James, the Armenian Patriarch takes his place on this revered throne.

The Golden Gate

This entrance into Jerusalem symbolizes the age-old diversity of religion and history in the region. Considered to be the original Gate Beautiful of Herod's time, it is also referred to by the Jews as the Gate of Mercy through which, according to tradition, the Messiah will one day pass on his way into Jerusalem. Christians believe that this already occurred two thousand years ago. And Muslims contend that this same gate is the Gate of Judgment referred to in the Koran. In AD 1187, after conquering Jerusalem, Saladin completely blocked this entrance. A Muslim cemetery was built in front of the gate in the belief that it would prevent the Jewish Messiah from entering the city.

< Via Dolorosa

Crosses and domes of the Franciscan Convent of the Flagellation overlook this arched pathway, believed to be the route taken by Jesus on his way to crucifixion. Via Dolorosa leads to the Church of the Holy Sepulchre. Every Friday, members of the Franciscan Church solemnly trace Jesus' route along the Via Dolorosa.

Jewish Quarter, Roman Ruins

While excavating at this site, an old Roman coin was found with the imprint of this street. The area was completely excavated, and the old Roman ruins and the street of the old Cardo were discovered and restored by Hebrew University archaeologists. Cardo, coming from the same root as the word *cardiac,* means *heart of the city.*

< Zion Gate

Battle scars from a siege in 1948 pockmark this entrance, known as the Gate of the Jewish Quarter. Leading to Mount Zion, the gate was constructed by Suleiman the Magnificent in the 16th century and was originally guarded by a gatekeeper with a key. Following the Six Day War, the bullet-riddled gate was opened to everyone and left as a graphic monument to history.

next page >
Western Wall

As the Western Wall loomed into view I stood captivated, unable to move as I collected my thoughts. Here is the most holy place in all Jewish religious and national consciousness. Millions of Jewish people, persecuted through the centuries, have dreamed of seeing this place. After setting up my easel, a group of about thirty schoolchildren surrounded me. Finding the colors of my painting attractive, one small girl told me she would like to eat them. An enthusiastic evangelist from Oklahoma regaled me with stories from the bible as he watched me paint. He was filled with love and knowledge of Jerusalem. The Western Wall, standing fifty feet high, is the last remnant of the Second Temple, which was destroyed by the Romans in AD 70. Its massive blocks of carved stone have been worn smooth by nineteen hundred years of weather, wind, and the touch of human hands. Rising beyond the wall is the Temple Mount—the Mount Moriah of biblical antiquity, where it is said Abraham prepared to slay Isaac, and where the First and Second temples once stood. The Temple Mount is now occupied by the Islamic Dome of the Rock and the silvery Al-Aksa Mosque.

Women at the Wall

The women at the Wall insert their prayers written on paper into its ancient cracks. They believe their prayers will go straight to God. Some spend hours in prayer and contemplation.

Israelis at the Western Wall

Israeli citizens prepare for the upcoming Independence Day celebration.

45

Bar Mitzvah at the Western Wall

Torah at the Western Wall

Cave inside the Western Wall

To the left of the Western Wall is a
dark tunnel that leads to excavations
under Wilson's Arch at the northern
corner of the Wall. Now a place of
study and prayer, this was part of the
Herodion Bridge, which once linked
the Temple Mount with the Jewish
Quarter. Inside I saw the original
Western Wall stones and more areas for
praying. The light inside the cave was
extraordinary, with golden-green hues
of an iridescent radiance.

The Dome of the Rock

Celebrating the glories of Islam, this striking mosque of marble, mosaic tile, stained glass, and inscriptions from the Koran is located on the Temple Mount, which Muslims call Haram esh-Sharif. Built in AD 692 by Caliph Abd Al-Malik, the Dome of the Rock sits on the site once occupied by the temples of Solomon and Herod. Beneath its gold-plated dome lies an immense boulder, named Kubbet es-Sakhra. This sacred rock is said to have been the one on which Abraham prepared his sacrifice of Isaac; it is the same rock from which Mohammed is believed to have ascended to heaven on his white horse.

Overlooking the Old City

Dung Gate

The past collides with the present at this ancient gate nearest the Western Wall. Having earned its rather unsavory name because of the refuse carted through it during the early Roman and Byzantine eras, the gate today swarms with snack stands, vendors, and Arab trinket merchants vying for tourist dollars amidst the din of taxi and bus traffic. There is even a camel available to pose with tourists.

Small Arab market

This picturesque market faces the bus stop near the Dung Gate, where I waited for a bus to get back to the center of the city. In the background is the Arab village of Silwan, where Solomon built temples to pagan gods who were worshiped by some of Solomon's one thousand wives, princesses, and concubines.

Mary's Tomb

Inside the Dormition Abbey, in the center of the circular crypt, rests a life-size statue of the sleeping Mary, made of cherry wood and ivory.

Room of the Last Supper

Located on Mount Zion above David's tomb is a bare room of vaulted arches known as the Cenacle. Here Jesus ate the Last Supper, or Passover seder, and taught his disciples the basic tenets of Christianity.

opposite >

Dormition Abbey

Erected on Mount Zion above the Old City, this towering Benedictine structure was built by Germans in 1910 to mark the location where Mary went to her eternal sleep. Noted for its impressive artwork, the interior offers a spacious circular prayer hall and a symbolic zodiac floor inscribed with the names of sixteen Prophets and the Twelve Apostles. Above the apse is an exquisite mosaic of Mary and the Baby Jesus.

The Church of All Nations

Two thousand years of history greet the eye from this vantage point near the foot of the Mount of Olives. The Church of All Nations, also known as the Basilica of Agony, sits in the foreground, its impressive Byzantine-style edifice resting atop ruins of a church built during the Crusades. Designed in 1926 by Antonio Barluzzi, the building's twelve graceful cupolas represent each of the twelve nations that donated funds for its construction. Adjoining the church is the Garden of Gethsemane, where Jesus prayed and was betrayed by Judas. Dominating the hillside in the distance are the onion domes of the Russian Church of Mary Magdalene. Built in the late 19th century by the Czar, the church is said to contain some of the hearts of the Romanov family.

The Russian Church of Mary Magdalene

This property of the Russian Church-in-exile was built by Czar Alexander III in 1885 in memory of his mother and is named after her saint.

The Lion's pool

Located in Bloomfield Park in the district of Yemin Moshe, the Lion's pool was a gift from German Chancellor Helmut Kohl to Teddy Kollek, the Mayor of Jerusalem.

next page >

View of the Wall from Bloomfield Park

An iron trellis covered with jasmine, morning glory, and other vines provided shade for me in Bloomfield Park, from which I painted the breathtaking view of the wall of the Old City.

Jerusalem Great Synagogue

Standing opposite the Jerusalem
Plaza Hotel on King George Street
is the Jerusalem Great Synagogue,
seat of the Chief Rabbinate in
Israel. Its 18th-century ark, which
covers the Torah Scrolls, was
transplanted from Padua, Italy.
And though this synagogue is of
modern design, it is built with the
same Jerusalem stone used
throughout the city.

YMCA

Built in 1933 by Arthur Loomis
Harmon, whose firm also helped design
New York City's Empire State Building,
the YMCA sits on a hill overlooking the
Old City, opposite the King David
Hotel. First established in Jerusalem in
1878 for young Christian men, the "Y" is
now open to everyone—Christians, Jews,
and Muslims of both sexes and all ages.
The facility's well-maintained flowered
terrace is a popular meeting place.

King David Hotel

I stopped for lunch at the stately King David Hotel. From my table, I looked out at the terrace brimming with beautiful flowers. I couldn't resist painting them. The maitre d' liked the painting so much he did not charge me for my lunch. The King David Hotel was built by Egyptian Jews in 1930 and was the British base of command during the Mandate period. One entire wing was destroyed by the Jewish underground in 1946. The hotel has been host to many world leaders, including Anwar Sadat, Jimmy Carter, and Henry Kissinger.

BEN YEHUDA STREET

Beginning at Zion Square and extending for five blocks is Ben Yehuda Street, the most popular mall in Jerusalem, jammed with outdoor restaurants, cafes, movie theaters, newsstands, and shops. They are always crowded with young people enjoying themselves, who come to meet their friends, be seen, and listen to the musicians in the street.

Ice cream in Jerusalem

Musicians in Ben Yehuda Street

Ben Yehuda Street on Friday

Sitting in the middle of the street closed to auto traffic, I painted the last-minute shoppers and strollers enjoying the balmy weather as others hurried to get home before the Sabbath.

Jerusalem on Saturday night

As sundown comes on Saturday, the people come out into the streets to celebrate the end of the Sabbath. Families and friends gather this night in Liberty Bell Park to eat, drink, and enjoy one another's company. Throughout the city the streets are alive with festivities.

Jerusalem wedding

Bus ride in Jerusalem

On a bus ride from the King David Hotel to Zion Square, I was able to sketch people seated near me.

Talpiot

While visiting friends in this neighborhood of Jerusalem, I was impressed by the design of this apartment complex. I especially liked the view looking out on the countryside.

Jerusalem train station

While painting this scene, the train pulled in from Haifa, obstructing my view. I returned the following day to finish the painting.

Mahane Yehuda market

Here in Jerusalem's main market, I overdosed on some of the best fruits and vegetables I have ever eaten.

next page >

Mea Shearim

On a warm day, I chased these three boys down the streets of Mea Shearim. I marveled at the dexterity of the boy balancing his large fur hat as he ran. Mea Shearim means *a hundred gates.* Populated by Hassidic Jews, these quarters were originally built in 1875 as a refuge for strictly observant Jewish families. Wearing the same style of clothing worn by their ancestors in 19th-century European shtetls, the Orthodox men don traditional black garments, fur hats, and sidecurls; the women wear simple shawls. Slight variations in dress and headgear can be seen in the different religious groups.

Avenue of the Righteous Among Nations

The six thousand trees planted here stand in honor of the six thousand heroic gentiles who risked their own lives to save Jews during the Holocaust. Among the honored is Raoul Wallenberg, the Swedish diplomat in Budapest who was personally responsible for rescuing thousands of Hungarian Jews from Third Reich annihilation. Wallenberg was never heard from after the Second World War ended.

The gateway to the Knesset

Created by Jerusalem sculptor David Palombo in 1960, the gateway to the Knesset is made of welded iron bars electroplated with steel to express the strength of the nation that fought with tenacity to achieve its aim of statehood.

The Great Menorah

Presented to the Knesset by the British Parliament in 1956, this inspiring sculpture stands as the ultimate symbol of the State of Israel. Created by Benno Alkan, its twenty-nine panels represent themes from Jewish history.

YAD VASHEM

Opened to the public in 1961, this unsettling memorial to the victims and survivors of the Holocaust stands as an eternal reminder of Nazi atrocities during the war. Preserved here are the names of more than three and a half million Jews who perished, and protected in a vault near the Eternal Light are the ashes of martyrs gathered from various Nazi death camps. Dark mirrored corridors lead through the Children's Memorial, where the names of the one and a half million children who died are illuminated by candlelight. The pain of the Holocaust is graphically preserved in the artwork of Jews persecuted during those days. Taken from the Book of Isaiah, Yad Vashem means *an everlasting memorial*.

When the world was upside down

The children in this painting are listening to their teacher tell them the story of the Holocaust in front of the famous sculptured panels by Naftali Bezem at the entrance of the museum. The first panel depicts the Holocaust; the second, Jewish resistance; the third, the pattern of the land of Israel; the fourth, rebirth of Israel as a nation.

King David's Tomb

Located on Mount Zion, this traditional burial place of Israel's great warrior-poet King David, who brought the Ark of the Covenant to his people, is considered one of the holiest sites in all of Israel. It is visited each year by multitudes of Jewish pilgrims. Located behind the tomb is the Chamber of the Holocaust, a haunting memorial to the millions of Jews slaughtered in Europe.

Tomb of Absalom

Facing the Temple Mount at the bottom of the Kidron Valley are the funerary monuments and buried caves of the Second Temple period. The most unusual is the Tomb of Absalom; the vast hole in the monument is attributed to grave robbers. Absalom, King David's rebellious son, died at the hands of his father's general. King David's lament, "Oh my son Absalom, my son Absalom! Would God I had died for thee," has become a classic expression of paternal grief.

Valley of the Cross

This valley is believed to mark the site of the tree from which the cross for Christ's crucifixion was made. Legend also has it that this tree was an offshoot of the Tree of Life that grew in the Garden of Eden. The Monastery of the Cross that dominates the area with its fortresslike exterior was a 6th-century Georgian monastery. It is now open to the public by the Greek Orthodox Church.

Carmit children's village

The Carmit school was created to provide disadvantaged children with good schooling, since their own homes and neighborhood environments are not conducive to developing their true potential. Many of the children suffer from neglect and learning deficiencies. A family-style framework has been set up for them at the school, which has lovely grounds and facilities. They are supervised with care by a group leader or house mother who lives with the children and encourages their activities. Carmit is one of the many educational facilities of the Histadrut, Israel's main health, education, and social institution.

Hillside of Ein Kerem

Ein Kerem

One of the loveliest places I visited in Israel is Ein Kerem, which means *spring of the vineyard*. It is the birthplace of John the Baptist. Some of its well-known sites are the Church of Visitation, Mary's Fountain, and the Church of St. John. On the hill above the village is the new Hadassah Hospital medical facility. Inside are the famed Marc Chagall stained-glass windows depicting the twelve tribes of Israel. With its charming vistas, Ein Kerem is reminiscent of the south of France. I long to return to paint the village again.

ALIYAH

The "ingathering of the exiles" brings people from around the world. The latest immigrants to be welcomed are the thousands of newcomers from the ancient Jewish community of Ethiopia, such as those pictured here at Mevasseret-Zion Absorption Center. The wave continues to grow with the arrival of thousands of Russians. Standing as a symbol of freedom and hope for people everywhere, the State of Israel opens its arms to all Jews coming home to the biblical land of their fathers.

opposite>

Kas Hadana

A chief Rabbi from Ethiopia, now residing at Mevasseret-Zion Absorption Center. The Ethiopian Jews are believed to be direct descendants of King Solomon and the Queen of Sheba of the tribe of Dan, one of the ten lost tribes dispersed by the Babylonians' conquest of the Kingdom of Judah.

Three Russian boys

Ethiopians at the Mevasseret-Zion Absorption Center

< Sheep and goats

At a crossing below St. Peter's Church in Galicanta, on the eastern slope of Mount Zion, the contrast between modern car traffic and age-old goat traffic was wonderful.

Greek Orthodox priest

Strolling through the Old City, I was impressed by this Greek Orthodox priest wearing sunglasses and a happy demeanor. Arriving with Alexander the Great in 333 BC, the Greek Orthodox Church is probably the oldest church in Jerusalem. It is certainly the most populous, possessing numerous religious communities, monasteries, and missions, and composed primarily of Arab-Christians.

The Russian compound

Designed to accommodate more than a thousand people, this imposing structure with its multiple domes and fortresslike walls was built in 1858 to house Russian immigrants. Contained within these walls are the Russian Orthodox Church, the Church of the Holy Trinity, the Jerusalem law courts, the Jerusalem police station, Herod's Pillar, and the Hall of Heroism where, during the British Mandate, many Jewish underground fighters were executed.

Bethlehem

*I*N THE JUDEAN HILLS LIES THE LITTLE TOWN OF BETHLEHEM, which means *house of bread.* It was a short trip by bus from Jerusalem, past ancient olive groves and Rachel's Tomb, to the town of Bethlehem, birthplace of Jesus. Sanctified by Christians throughout the world, Bethlehem contains many monasteries and churches, the most sacred being the Basilica of the Nativity. Built in the 4th century by the Emperor Constantine, the church sits over the cave where Jesus was born. Nearby is Ruth's Field and Shepherds' Field, where the Angel appeared before the shepherds to announce the birth of Christ. Located at the top of a few stairs on Manger Road are three cisterns, known as David's Wells. It was here that water was brought to David during his battle with the Philistines. And a short distance to the east is Herodion, Herod's awesome citadel, which rises majestically from the Judean Desert floor. Today, Bethlehem is populated mainly by Arab-Christians.

< *St. Catherine's Church*

St. Catherine's Church was originally built in 1882. Having fallen into disrepair over the years, it was restored in 1948. Today's church has a beautiful Crusader cloister with a garden and towering palms. Dominating the center of this serene courtyard is a statue of St. Jerome; next to the statue, symbolizing his austere life, is a skull.

Bethlehem

Birthplace of David and Jesus

A CHRONOLOGY

PRE-CHRISTIAN ERA

1830 BC—Rachel dies on the way to Bethlehem and is buried near Bethlehem.

1004 BC—Center of the tribe of Judah; place of worship of the Lord.

1000 BC—Samuel appoints David King in Bethlehem.

735–722 BC—Babylonian conquest and Jewish exile. Exiles return to Bethlehem.

CHRISTIAN ERA

AD 1—Christ is born in a manger in a cave east of the city.

132–135—Roman garrison, stationed in Bethlehem, roots out the second Jewish revolt against Rome, led by Bar-Kochba.

326—Emperor Constantine of Byzantium makes Christianity the official religion of the Empire.

1009–1100—First Crusade. Bethlehem is seized by the Crusaders. The first kings of the Latin Kingdom, Baldwin I and II, are crowned in the Church of the Nativity.

1149—Fall of the Latin Kingdom.

1489—Fort built by Crusaders is demolished and city is inhabited by a Christian majority of different denominations.

1837—Earthquake and fire destroy most of the Church of the Nativity.

1847—The Silver Star, taken from the Bethlehem Basilica, is one of the factors leading to the outbreak of the Crimean War.

1933—The Church of the Nativity is partially restored by the British Mandate government.

1948–1949—St. Catherine Crusader Cloister is restored.

1962–1964—All the caves connecting the Grotto of the Nativity are restored. They are discovered to be pre-Byzantine caves.

Inside St. Catherine's Cathedral

326—Constantine and his mother build the Church of the Nativity over the cave where Jesus was born.

386—Saint Jerome translates the bible from the original Hebrew into Latin. Known as the Vulgate, this is still the official bible of the Roman Catholic Church.

529—The Church of the Nativity is destroyed during the Samaritan uprising against Byzantine rule, but is rebuilt by Justinian and becomes known as the Basilica of the Nativity.

614—Persians conquer Bethlehem, but spare the Church of the Nativity because of the adoration of Jesus by kings in Oriental costumes portrayed over the church.

June 1967—Bethlehem surrenders to the Israeli army without a fight, typical of its charmed life through the ages of having been spared by almost all invaders: Romans, Byzantines, Arabs, Crusaders, Mamelukes, and Turks.

1967—After the Six Day War, Bethlehem comes under Israeli administration. All the holy shrines are open to everyone.

1967–1992—Bethlehem today is most celebrated on Christmas Eve. From all over the world, a choir gathers to perform outside the Church of the Nativity. St. Catherine's Church, adjacent to the Church of the Nativity, celebrates Christmas Eve with a worldwide broadcast of its midnight mass.

Rachel's Tomb

One of the most sacred spots in all of Israel, this unimposing tomb is located on the road from Jerusalem to Bethlehem. Believed to be the burial site of Jacob's wife, Rachel, the tomb is revered as a place of worship. Its simple dome was built in 1841 by Sir Moses Montefiore to commemorate the place where Jacob "set a pillar upon her grave."

Christian Mission Church

One of the many churches, monasteries, and religious places that greet you on the road in Bethlehem.

Main street in Bethlehem

Manger Square

Although there were few people
around at the time of this painting,
Manger Square—opposite the
Church of the Nativity—is
crowded with the procession of
celebrants at Christmas and Easter.

The Church of the Nativity

Visitors to this revered Christian
landmark must stoop to enter its
low doorway, which was reduced
in size for defensive purposes
during the Crusades. Built over
the remains of an earlier Byzantine
church, the simple, rough-hewn
exterior belies the exquisite mosaics within. The original basilica,
constructed by the Emperor
Constantine in AD 305, was built
over the cave where, it is said,
Jesus was born.

The Chapel of the Manger

In the Grotto of the Nativity, next to the Silver Star on the floor to mark the place of Jesus' birth, is the Chapel of the Manger. This is where Mary placed the newborn infant. Praying in this golden light are two people who realized their life's dream with their pilgrimage to the Chapel of the Manger.

Beersheba

LOCATED SIXTY-EIGHT MILES SOUTH OF TEL AVIV, Beersheba was a sleepy Arab settlement. In 1948, during the birth of the State of Israel, this settlement suddenly sprang up like a frontier boomtown to support the growing number of immigrants pouring in from over seventy-five countries. Today, at Beersheba's Ben Gurion University, a world-renowned veterinary hospital boasts a one-of-a-kind "camel clinic" for the Bedouin, and the facility has gained a solid reputation for breeding championship Arabian horses. Mentioned often in the bible, Beersheba is where Elijah fled to avoid Jezebel's wrath, and where Samuel sent his sons to be judges. Isaac, Joshua, and Jacob also passed through this historic locale. Meaning *seven wells* in Hebrew, and also known as the *Well of the Oath*, Beersheba was named in memory of an ancient covenant between the patriarch Abraham and Abimelech, the local ruler of the time, who allowed Abraham to water his flocks here.

Bedouins at lunch in the desert

Beersheba

Southernmost city
of the Kingdom of Judah

A CHRONOLOGY

CHALCOLITHIC ERA–LATE BRONZE AGE: 4500–1200 BC

4500–3100 BC—Cave dwellers raise cattle, make metal tools, and live in subterranean dwellings, protected from enemies and the desert.

1970 BC—Abraham and Isaac dig wells and form alliances with Abimelech, King of the Philistines. Abraham sets aside seven ewes, which gives the city its name: *sheva* (seven) or *shevua* (oath).

1900 BC—Twelve Tribes of Israel conquer Canaan. Isaac and Jacob encamp near Beersheba, where caravans ply trade routes between Egypt and Arabia.

1700? BC—Beersheba is assigned to the tribe of Shimeon and is later incorporated under the tribe of Judah.

IRON AGE: 1200–586 BC

1200–1100 BC—Beersheba is a religious-administrative center in the time of Samuel. Samuel sends his sons, Joel and Abiah, to sit as judges in Beersheba, but their corruption sparks a popular demand for a monarchy. This leads to crowning Saul King.

EARLY ROMAN ERA: 63 BC–AD 300

AD 70—Beersheba is in the Roman frontier defense line and fights the Nabateans.

LATE ROMAN AND BYZANTINE ERAS: 300–638

300–400—A synagogue and a Byzantine church are built in Beersheba.

400–500—Beersheba is annexed to "Palestina Tertia."

OTTOMAN ERA: 1517–1917

1900—Turkish government sets up an administrative district in Beersheba in its struggle against Britain over the delineation of Egypt's border in Sinai.

WORLD WAR I–POST–WORLD WAR II ERA: 1914–1948

1914–1918—City is a base for the Turko-German army fighting in Sinai and on the Suez.

1917—General Allenby seizes Beersheba with Australian and New Zealand units.

1922–1939—Of the 98 Jews, only 11 remain here after the Arab riots.

1947—The Egyptian army makes its head-quarters here. U.N. awards most of area to Israel.

MODERN ISRAEL ERA: 1948–PRESENT

1948—The Israeli army conquers the city during the War of Independence.

1948–1962—New settlers from Eastern Europe, South America, and Arab countries make their home in Beersheba, which is also a market center for Negev Bedouins.

Thursday's Bedouin market

900 BC—Prophet Elijah seeks refuge in Beersheba from the wrath of Queen Jezebel, pagan wife of King Ahab, who seeks to kill Elijah for slaying 400 prophets of Ba'al. In this era of a divided monarchy, by fleeing to Beersheba in Judah, Elijah is beyond the reach of the rulers of Israel.

600 BC—Jewish exiles from Babylonian captivity settle in Beersheba and the city prospers.

1969—Ben Gurion University of the Negev is established. Excavations uncover a great fortified city from King David's time.

1973—David Ben Gurion is buried in Kibbutz Sde Boker, together with his wife, Paula. Beersheba Municipal Theater founded.

Ethiopians in Beersheba

The Ethiopian immigrants in
Beersheba have joined with native-
born Israelis and immigrants from
all over the world to make
Beersheba a vital and fascinating city
of more than 100,000 inhabitants.

The Dead Sea

Lying more than four hundred meters below
sea level, this ancient body of water—actually
a lake—is the lowest place on earth, and
certainly the saltiest. The Dead Sea draws
visitors from around the world who come to
experience the mystical and rejuvenating
powers believed to exist in its waters. These
Bedouins were selling ducks in the desert near
the Dead Sea.

next page >

The Bedouin market

Bedouin women, dressed in traditional black velvet, sit in the intense
heat of the desert day surrounded by bolts of brightly colored fabrics
and clothes for sale. Every Thursday the Bedouin still trade their
sheep, camels, and goats here and sell hand-woven rugs, keffiye
headdresses, silks, jewelry, camel saddles, spices, and Bedouin arts
and crafts. I was particularly fascinated by the symbolic blue tattoos
on the backs of some of the women's hands and also between their
lower lips and chins. These tattoos indicate the tribe to which these
women belong. Though they did not appreciate being looked at by
strangers, I was determined to work in their midst.

Rising majestically from the Judean Desert on the western shores of the Dead Sea, Masada represents one of the most tragic yet inspiring events in the history of Israel. It was nearly twenty centuries ago atop this mountain—the last Jewish stronghold after the fall of Jerusalem in AD 70—that a band of Jewish freedom fighters surrounded by thousands of Roman soldiers fiercely held out against a siege lasting four years. Constructing colossal ramps, fifteen thousand Roman soldiers eventually managed to storm the summit, where they discovered that all 960 men, women, and children had committed suicide rather than submit to Roman slavery. The massive quantities of food and water left behind by the deceased Jews were intended as a clear message to the victors: "We prefer death to enslavement." Symbolizing freedom today, Masada is used for numerous official and religious ceremonies. When recruits of the Israeli Defense Forces' Armored Unit swear their allegiance during the annual ceremony on the summit, they recite the following oath: "Masada shall not fall again. We shall remain free." Bar mitzvahs are also regularly performed here. A favorite campsite for tourists, with a spectacular view, the fortresslike summit can be reached by cable car or on foot along the Snake Path that ascends the eastern face above the Dead Sea and the Judean wilderness. Greeting you at the top is the incredible three-tiered palace of Herod the Great. Vast storerooms, terraces, synagogues, a 5th-century Byzantine chapel, a swimming pool, a Roman bath house, the mosaic floors of the Western Palace, and the sacred Mikve make Masada a fascinating place to visit.

This ritual bath, built in the era of the Second Temple, was constructed in accordance with strict Jewish religious law. The defenders of Masada were devout Jews. Rainwater was collected in one pool and stored. The second pool was the actual bath used for immersion. The third pool, which is not connected to the others, is the smallest and was used for washing hands and feet before a person immersed in the Mikve.

Hills of the Negev

Beneath a towering tabletop mountain, Bedouin flocks graze on rolling grasslands where Abraham once tended his flocks. Nearby, the black tents of the ancient Atyek Bedouin tribe rise against the backdrop of modern-day Beersheba and bustling kibbutzim. Here, on the boundary between northern and southern Negev, vegetation comes to an abrupt end, now replaced by the cratered, rock-strewn desolation of the southern Negev Desert. This barren expanse of no-man's-land extends down through the Sinai, all the way to Eilat, where the southern tip of Israel meets the Red Sea—the place where Moses first stood after his exodus from Egypt.

Eilat

Located on the northern coast of the Red Sea and perched directly between Jordan and the Egyptian Sinai Peninsula, Eilat is Israel's southernmost city. Serving as the country's summer resort in winter, Eilat is known for its rich underwater life and exceptional snorkeling. From the incredible Coral World Observatory below sea level, visitors can observe magnificent rainbow-hued fish darting around the sea plants and coral.

Glass bottom boat

Water's edge in Eilat

< *King Solomon's Pillars*

In the wilderness of the Negev Desert in Timna Park are Solomon's Pillars, natural formations of Nubian sandstone. Colored in varying tones of pink, yellow, white, and purple, these huge sentinels have been polished by centuries of wind and sand. Nearby are the copper mines, believed to be King Solomon's, of three thousand years ago.

Tel Aviv

THE PEOPLE I MET IN TEL AVIV WERE THE MOST cosmopolitan in Israel. Two Israeli friends, Ahuva and Yifrach, exemplified the warmth and good nature of this city's inhabitants. They opened their house and shared their friends, ideas, and time with me. Yifrach drove me to the original section of Tel Aviv where he was born, with its old houses, schools, and reconstruction, past the Hassan Bek Mosque and down to Jaffa Bay, to paint the fishermen as they came in from their morning catch. Tel Aviv sprang into existence in 1909 when a group of Jewish residents from Jaffa, tired of the noise and overcrowded conditions of the city, decided to virtually create their own quiet garden community, a place of peace and respite after a hectic day. Purchasing a desolate strip of sand dunes near Jaffa, they divided up the land by lottery. Almost overnight rose the first new Jewish city in over two thousand years. In Hebrew, a *tel* is an artificial hill built over the accumulated rubble of the past, while *aviv* means *spring,* or *new life*. Tel Aviv was born. And it flourished. In 1950 it officially merged with Jaffa to form the greater city of Tel Aviv-Jaffa. Considered Israel's first modern city, Tel Aviv is a bustling cultural, artistic, and business center with parks, zoos, museums, beaches, theaters, and world-renowned orchestras.

Panoramic view of Tel Aviv from the Sheraton Hotel

Tel Aviv

First all-Jewish city in modern times

A CHRONOLOGY

PRE-CHRISTIAN ERA

4500–3100 BC—Stone-Bronze age. Chalcolithic remains. Pottery and ossuaries shaped like miniature homes uncovered by Israeli archaeologists in the 20th century.

1700 BC—Hyksos settlement. Excavated on south bank of Yarkon River in 1927 by archaeologist E. Sukenik.

1100 BC—Philistine settlement.

1000–520 BC—Discovery of the remains of Jewish settlements from times of David, Solomon, the kings of Israel, and the returning Babylonian exiles, who flourished here. Earlier remains of Canaanite and Philistine settlements also discovered. Trade with Phoenicia.

520 BC—Return of exiles. City rebuilt at Tel Kasile, on the Yarkon River.

CHRISTIAN ERA

AD 1260–1517—Mameluke period. Glazed pottery excavated at Tel Kasile.

1799—Napoleon's forces use the Yarkon river as a rest camp.

1909—Tel Aviv, "Hill of Spring," is founded. It is a symbol of Ezekiel's vision.

1930—Tel Aviv becomes Israel's largest urban settlement.

1937—Remains of a fort built in 950 BC, in the days of Solomon, found at Tel Kedadi near today's Hilton and Sheraton hotels.

May 14, 1948—State of Israel proclaimed in Tel Aviv Museum building. With independence, Tel Aviv thrives as a commercial, financial, tourist, and cultural center. Hellenistic, Roman, and Byzantine remains uncovered.

1950—Tel Aviv merges with Jaffa.

1965—Tel Aviv University established as a unified institution.

1979—Beth Hatefutsoth Museum of the Jewish Diaspora founded.

1991—Iraqi scud missiles damage Tel Aviv in Gulf War.

Hassan Bek Mosque

This mosque was built in 1916 by the Turkish-Arab governor, Hassan Bek, and has come to signify the border between Tel Aviv and Jaffa. During the Israeli War of Independence, the mosque was used as an Arab sniper outpost.

Gordon and Dizengoff Streets

There was heavy pedestrian traffic while I was painting at this corner. Like a Paris street with outdoor cafes and shops, the upbeat mood of the people was hard to resist. So were the shops with jewelry, leather goods, and Gottex bathing suits!

Kings of Israel Square

Facing City Hall with its memorial sculpture for the Holocaust in the foreground.

Susan Dallal Cultural Center

Tel Aviv washing

Asia House and the IBM Building

Seeming to undulate like huge horizontal waves, the multitiered exterior of the Asia House is considered the most unique architectural edifice in Tel Aviv. Looming next door is the massive three-sided IBM building.

Jaffa

ONE OF THE OLDEST CITIES IN THE WORLD, RICH IN legend, the ancient port of Jaffa is where Noah's son Japheth made his home after Noah's ark came to rest atop Mount Ararat. Impressed by the pristine beauty of the area, Japheth named it Yafo, which means *beautiful* in Hebrew. This is where Jonah the Prophet is believed to have boarded the ship for Tarshish, only to be swallowed by the whale, and where the Apostle Peter miraculously raised Tabitha from the dead. It was also here, according to Greek mythology, that the beautiful Andromeda was chained to a rock over treacherous waters and later saved from a sea monster by Perseus astride his winged steed. Napoleon's armies came here, conquered the Turks, and died in vast numbers when a plague swept the city. Modern-day Jaffa is a place where the past and present blend comfortably; where local fishermen still bring in their daily catch in the age-old tradition of their fathers; and where contemporary artists' studios, galleries, shops, and trendy restaurants occupy ancient winding streets. In 1950, Jaffa merged with its neighbor, Tel Aviv. While here, I visited composer Dov Seltzer and his designer wife, Graziella, in their exquisite home overlooking Jaffa Harbor. Colored stones are inlaid in the floors of their home, and arches frame the view as you watch the ships at sea. We sipped drinks on the roof garden, which was overflowing with flowers. The conversation was so stimulating that I never got around to painting the house!

The Arab section

Down the winding hill to the older Arab section of Jaffa, kiosks and open-air cafes abound with sweet pastries and food. The bread I bought at an Arab bakery, fresh from its primitive oven, was delicious. The ancient streets were filled with shoppers and the atmosphere was warm and friendly.

Jaffa

Japheth, son of Noah, named it Yafo. The Greeks link it with Jopa, daughter of Aeolius, ruler of the winds.

A CHRONOLOGY

PRE-CHRISTIAN ERA

1800–1600 BC—First fortified settlement.

1500–1450 BC—Jaffa is conquered by Pharaoh Tuthmose II.

1200–1000 BC—Israelites settle near the Sea People and the Philistines.

960 BC—King Solomon ships in cedars from Lebanon for the construction of the Temple.

701 BC—Jaffa is conquered by Assyrian King Sennacherib.

586–332 BC—Jaffa under Persian rule. Jewish exiles return from Babylon, and again cedars are imported for building the Second Temple. Darius cedes Jaffa to Sidonese King Eshmunazzar. It becomes a Phoenician colony. Jonah flees to Jaffa to board a ship and is swallowed by the whale.

152 BC—Hellenistic city under Ptolemaic and Seleucid rule. Greek legend of Andromeda is set at this time.

144–142 BC—Simon the Maccabee liberates Jaffa, making it a major port for the Hasmonean dynasty and the Herodion era.

CHRISTIAN ERA

AD 70—Because of Caesarea's loyalty to the Hasmoneans under King Herod, Jaffa is bypassed by Herod's construction of Caesarea's port.

324—Israel comes under Byzantine rule. Massacres against Jews.

40–1099—Mamelukes control Eretz Israel and Jaffa becomes a major port again.

1100–1200—Jaffa serves as a port for the Crusader Kingdom of Jerusalem.

1200–1300—Jaffa is destroyed, with all other Crusader ports, by the Mamelukes.

1515—Conquest by Ottoman Sultan Salim launches 400 years of Turkish rule.

1600–1800—Christian institutions and Jewish community established.

1799—Napoleon conquers Jaffa. Bubonic plague breaks out. Napoleon leaves for Egypt after his defeat at Akko.

1832–1842—Egypt's Mohammed Ali conquers Jaffa, but Turks defeat him within a decade.

1892–1900—Jerusalem-Jaffa railway and Jaffa clock tower are built.

1917—Turks expel Jews from Tel Aviv-Jaffa. British forces of General Allenby conquer Jaffa.

1936–1939—Anti-Jewish riots. Many Jewish casualties. Port is closed to Jewish immigration.

May 14, 1948—Jaffa is liberated during Passover by underground Hagannah and Irgun Zvai Leumi forces, on the eve of Israel's independence.

April 1950—Unified Tel Aviv-Jaffa municipality established.

1963—Extensive artists' quarter created amidst ancient streets.

1992—Ancient harbor and historic places restored as a leading cultural center.

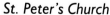

St. Peter's Church

Located in the courtyard of this beautiful Franciscan church is the St. Louis Monastery, named after the French King who led a Crusade here in 1147. Centuries later, Napoleon stayed here after conquering Jaffa.

Morning catch at Jaffa Harbor

One of the oldest harbors in the
world, Jaffa Harbor at seven in the
morning was alive with fishermen
bringing in their day's catch.

Jaffa port and lighthouse

Reconstructed in 1963, the Jaffa lighthouse stands watch over this colorful maze of shops, galleries, nightclubs, and popular seafood restaurants. Fresh Mediterranean breezes made this beautiful locale a favorite spot of mine.

The art colony labyrinth

Aladin Cafe

At the entrance to the Old City of Jaffa is the romantic Aladin Cafe, with the best view of Jaffa Harbor and the Tel Aviv skyline. Lunching with friends on a perfect day, we watched the seagulls and the boats on the water.

Netanya

Nestled in the biblical Plain of Sharon between Tel Aviv and Caesarea, this unique Mediterranean beach resort is renowned as the diamond cutting and polishing center of the world.

School's out in Netanya

Ballooning by the sea

Light breezes and clifftop vistas enhance the beauty of this exquisitely landscaped promenade. Nearby, a stairway descends to eight separate beaches, where breakwaters divide the area into gentle bays.

Cityscape of Netanya

Caesarea

ENTERING THE VAULTED CRUSADER GATE HOUSE and crossing the bridge over a wide moat, I was captivated by these interconnected and mysterious arches. Caesarea, with its restaurants and shops overlooking the Mediterranean Sea, was an unexpected delight. Feeling as though time stood still, I explored the ruins and painted the scene. Named in honor of Caesar Augustus, this Mediterranean port city is considered one of the finest examples of Roman and Crusader architecture in all of Israel. It was built in 20 BC by Herod the Great after Caesar had confirmed him King of Judea. I journeyed back in history as I viewed the city's ancient walls, splendid excavated ruins, and the Roman amphitheater where captives were paraded in triumph before being fed to wild beasts. Today, the amphitheater is used for open-air concerts. Rising from the sea are massive Roman pillars, placed here over two thousand years ago. Just outside Caesarea is the Street of Statues, lined with the unsettling forms of headless Roman dignitaries. A Roman aqueduct winds along the beach, where children search for old coins buried in the sand.

Crusader's Arches

These impressive arches are found in the
Hall of the Crusader Main Gate.

Caesarea

A CHRONOLOGY

PRE-CHRISTIAN ERA

300–200 BC—Captured by Phoenicians, who build an anchorage here for their naval colonies and name it Straton's Tower.

104–96 BC—King Alexander Jannai incorporates it into the Hasmonean Kingdom. Settlement of Jews.

22 BC—Caesar Augustus confirms Herod as King of Judea and Herod shows his gratitude by building a monument to his patron, Caesar, naming it Caesarea.

10 BC—Herod inaugurates the most striking leading maritime city in the eastern Mediterranean. Palaces in white stone adorn the city as do Caesar's palace, the amphitheater, temples, public buildings, a marketplace, and deep-sea harbor. Outside the city walls, Herod builds the Hippodrome for Caesar's "games."

4 BC—King Herod dies.

CHRISTIAN ERA

AD 6—Caesarea becomes the seat of Judea's Roman Procurators.

66—Jews of Caesarea revolt against the Romans and its Roman general Vespasian. Riots between the Jews and Caesarea's Syrians lead Vespasian to side with the Syrians. The Jews fight them both. Some 20,000 Jews are massacred. This touches off the Great Jewish War which ends four years later with the fall of Jerusalem and the destruction of the Second Temple. With Jerusalem razed, Caesarea becomes the capital of Palestine for almost 500 years.

October 4, 70—Titus celebrates his victory with "games" in the amphitheater in which 2,500 Jewish prisoners perish, are fed to the lions, or are shipped to Rome into slavery.

70–300—Jews return to Caesarea and build synagogues and schools. Early Christianity develops here: Apostle Peter baptizes Centurion Cornelius; Paul is imprisoned here and is later sent to Rome.

135—The great sage and spiritual leader Rabbi Akiva is martyred here by the Romans after the failed Bar-Kochba uprising.

639—Arab conquest. Caesarea remains opulent, but Herod's splendid harbor falls into decay.

1101—King Baldwin I, with the help of the Genoese fleet, captures Caesarea.

1187—The Saracens, under Saladin, recapture Caesarea. For 40 years, it changes hands five times between Arabs and Christians.

1228—Caesarea returns to Christian control.

1251—Louis IX of France, at the end of the Crusaders' exploits, builds the "impregnable" fortifications and moat, uncovered in later excavations.

1291—The Sultan Beibars captures Caesarea, which fades into obscurity under sand dunes.

1864—Muslim refugees from Bosnia settle here.

1948–1962—Baron James de Rothchild builds a home here. Israeli archaeologists uncover the Crusader City, the Hippodrome, the Byzantine Street of Statues, the Roman aqueduct, and the Roman amphitheater, where world-renowned artists perform in summer musical and theatrical festivals. Israel's first golf course opens.

1985—Underwater excavations uncover a temple dedicated to Caesar Augustus and the Goddess Roma, buried beneath a huge Byzantine church in the sea.

Breakwater

Overview of Caesarea

From my precarious vantage point atop excavated ruins, I leaned my painting pad against an ancient stone. Looking down, I was able to paint this vast scene of Caesarea, King Herod's gift to Caesar. In my view were the uncovered moats and pathways leading to the restored Crusader fortifications constructed partly with the remnants of Roman and Byzantine buildings, and the harbor filled with small sailboats. Within the breakwater, children were happily swimming and fishing in the shimmering Mediterranean Sea. While I was working, my French-speaking driver amused himself by singing popular French songs. We were later joined by two novitiate nuns who climbed up the excavation to enjoy the view.

Haifa

O N MAY 14, ISRAEL'S INDEPENDENCE DAY, I SPENT the afternoon with my paints in Mother's Garden, the biggest of Haifa's four hundred parks. The Arab and Jewish children got along very well, playing together. And their parents were on friendly terms, too. It was a charming park with playgrounds and food for the many people there that day. Haifa is Israel's third largest city and port. Located at the base of the steep Carmel mountain range, Haifa is Israel's premiere maritime center, its port highly valued as a Mediterranean haven for eighteen centuries. But Haifa's impact on human history goes back much further. Discovered in caves to the south of the city in the late 1920s were the skeletal remains of Early Man, dating back some thirty thousand years! Mentioned in Solomon's "Song of Songs," Mount Carmel offered me this spectacular view from my balcony at the Dan Carmel Hotel. The panorama was so magnificent that after painting it, I stayed to watch the Independence Day fireworks shooting all over the mountain and vanishing into the sea.

Haifa

View from my balcony at the Dan Carmel Hotel on the slopes of Mount Carmel overlooking the Bahai Temple and the harbor.

Haifa
A CHRONOLOGY

PRE-CHRISTIAN ERA

1300–1400 BC—The earliest settlement near Haifa is a small port town established in the Late Bronze Age, existing until the Hellenistic Era.

965–932 BC—Mount Carmel, mentioned in Solomon's "Song of Songs," is the scene of the Prophet Elijah's conflict with the pagan priests of the Ba'al, in the days of Ahab and Jezebel.

520 BC—Returning Jewish exiles from Babylon settle here.

333–63 BC—Hellenistic Era. The city is moved southward.

63 BC–AD 326—Roman Era. Jews bury their dead in caves.

CHRISTIAN ERA

AD 500—Isfia Synagogue, with mosaic floor depicting candelabra and Jewish ritual objects, reveals the inscription *Shalom el Yisreal*—Peace be unto Israel.

628–1100—Byzantine conquest. Destruction of the Jewish community. Crusaders besiege Haifa and seize it with the aid of the Venetian navy, killing most of the city's Jewish defenders.

1187—The fortress of Haifa is destroyed as Saladin deals a crushing blow to Crusader rule.

1192–1265—Haifa is returned to the Franks during the Third Crusade.

1250–1265—France's Louis IX rebuilds Haifa's fortifications, but it again falls to the Mameluke Sultan Beibars, who drives the Crusaders out and razes Haifa.

1291—The Carmelite Monastery, founded by the Mount Carmel Order in 1156, is destroyed by the Muslims.

1516—Ottoman conquest. Haifa is a half-ruined, impoverished village.

1600–1700—Haifa revives as a flourishing port, with immigration of Jews from Turkey, North Africa, and Europe.

1799—Napoleon uses the Carmelite Monastery as a hospital.

1924—Technion Institute of Technology opens.

1928–1934—Skeletons of an intermediate type between Neanderthal man and *Homo sapiens* are found by an Anglo-American expedition in caves south of Haifa on the Carmel range.

1936–1939—Arab riots adversely affect Haifa's economy.

1948—The British leave and the Hagannah captures the Arab quarter and takes over Haifa.

1959—Subway opens.

1963—Haifa University is founded.

1980—Port expanded and modernized.

1992—Haifa becomes the American 6th Fleet's favorite port in the Middle East.

1992—Technion has a new drug for Parkinson's disease, and an environmental pollution reduction by an aerodynamic sprayer, and a laser which can extract gas from oil shale. Technion also has developed a synthetic artificial blood material based on charcoal compatible with all blood groups and stockpiled without refrigeration.

Mother's Garden

Rice

Bahai shrine and gardens >

Tree-lined walks, spacious lawns, and lush gardens enhance the beauty of this sacred Bahai Temple on the slopes of Mount Carmel. Founded in 19th-century Persia by Mirza Ali Mohammed, who lies entombed beneath its dome, the Bahai religion is based on the universal brotherhood of charity and love, its members being spiritual disciples of Moses, Jesus, Buddha, and Mohammed, all "messengers sent to God." Today, the majority of the Bahai faith's members reside in the United States.

DRUZE VILLAGES OF ISFIYA AND DALIYAT EL CARMEL

Atop a mountain south of Haifa, shopkeepers do brisk business with busloads of tourists who come to buy the finely crafted carpets, baskets, and other handmade goods produced by these ancient and secretive people. Claiming direct lineage to Jethro, the father-in-law of Moses, whose shrine is in the Valley of Kfar Hittim in Galilee, the enigmatic Druze have preserved their own separate religious faith for centuries. The secrets of the faith are stubbornly protected by sheiks and religious leaders; in fact, most of the Druze are themselves unaware of these secrets and choose simply to obey without question the strict moral tenets they are taught. Tending to inhabit the most inaccessible areas in the hills of Galilee and the Carmel mountains, the seventy thousand Druze have been persecuted in the Middle East ever since they rejected mainstream Islam in the 11th century, and instead accepted the self-proclaimed divinity of the Egyptian Caliph El Hakim Abu Ali el-Mansur. Being fiercely loyal Israeli citizens, young Druze proudly serve with the Israeli Defense Forces. Many of them are decorated for their service and bravery in the regular army, armored corps, reconnaissance units, paratroops, and border police.

Druze house

Akko

A PROFUSION OF DOMES AND MINARETS OVERLOOKS this historical Mediterranean city, one of the oldest inhabited seaport cities in the world and one of the last two Christian strongholds at the end of the Crusades. Also known as St. Jean d'Acre, it was here that, in 1799, Napoleon terminated his failed two-month siege of the city, ending forever his eastern campaign. Akko was a charming and dramatic place to visit. I found it exciting to paint on the same streets where the art of glasswork had been born—streets traveled by Alexander the Great in the 4th century and where, three hundred years later, Julius Caesar walked. After exploring the subterranean Crusader City with its medieval rooms, I entered the open inner square with sunlight sparkling through the arches. An arrogant, handsome young Arab horseman suddenly appeared out of nowhere, riding bareback. Proudly prancing his horse in front of me, he circled the area and disappeared.

The harbor clock tower

Built in 1906, this rectangular Turkish clock tower presides over the khan el-Umdan, or Inn of Columns.

Akko (ACRE)

One of the world's oldest cities

A CHRONOLOGY

PRE-CHRISTIAN ERA

1800 BC—Ancient Akko appears in Egyptian Execution text and later in the records of Seti and Rameses II.

1600 BC (approx.)—Akko is allotted to the tribe of Asher, who is unable to subdue it. Akko remains an independent Phoenician city.

1468 BC—Akko is one of the cities conquered by Tuthmose III and is later mentioned in the El-Amarna letters, with King Zurata of Akko allying himself with Jerusalem.

965–932 BC—King Solomon imports his Sicilian horses through Akko.

538–333 BC—Persian rule. Akko is a vital military and naval base in the campaigns against Egypt.

312 BC—Ptolemy I reoccupies Akko.

300 BC—Akko, derived from the Greek word *ake* for "healing," has its name changed to Ptolemais by Ptolemy II, a Macedonian King.

350–200 BC—Greek coins, in gold and silver, are struck in Akko.

164–143 BC—Simeon the Hasmonean repulses the Seleucid (Arab) attacks.

71 BC—Akko passes from Cleopatra Selene to Armenia.

48 BC—After Pompey's occupation of the country, Caesar lands here.

39 BC—Herod makes Akko a base for his conquest of the country.

CHRISTIAN ERA

AD 66—Jewish War breaks out. Two thousand of Akko's Jews are massacred.

70 (approx.)—Nero makes Akko a Roman colony, renaming it Colonia Claudia Ptolemais Ghermanica.

100—Jews reestablish their community after the war against Rome.

614–628—Jews fight the Byzantines.

1104—Baldwin I, Crusader King of Jerusalem, seizes Akko.

1187—The Saracens, under Saladin, seize Akko from the Crusaders.

1189–1191—England's Richard the Lionheart, France's Philip Augustus, and Guy de Lusignan, successor to King Baldwin IV as King of Jerusalem, return Akko to Crusader control. For one century, Akko is the Crusaders' capital. They build fortresses and a subterranean city for the Knights of St. John.

1211–1300—Rabbis from France and England arrive to settle here.

1291—Akko falls to the Mamelukes.

1775—Ottoman ruler Ahmed Al-Jazzar rebuilds Akko and its Roman-style aqueduct.

1799—Napoleon besieges Akko, unsuccessfully. The British fleet helps Al-Jazzar to defend the city.

1832—Ibrahim, son of Egypt's Mohammed Ali, takes Akko and fortifies it.

1840—Akko is destroyed by Turkish rule.

1919—British takeover.

1938–1947—Jewish underground fighters are imprisoned in the Akko prison—the Crusader fortress. Shlomo Ben Yosef, Dov Gruner, and other members of the Irgun go to the gallows.

1948—New immigrants arrive.

1991—Moslem and Christian Arabs, Bahais, Druzes, and Jews live together in harmony.

Children playing

The empty caverns of this ancient aqueduct provide the setting for children as they play marbles.

The lighthouse

Overlooking the Mediterranean
from the western end of Akko Bay,
this lighthouse—also called the
Tower of Flies—is perched atop
fortifications built by the Crusaders.

View of the fortress

Arriving from Haifa, I stopped to have lunch with my driver, David, in full view of the magnificent fortress built by Al-Jazzar, which I later painted. The fortress was used as an arsenal during Turkish times and is the prison where Mirza Ali Mohammed, founder of the Bahai faith, was incarcerated by the Turks. It is also the site of the execution of Jewish underground fighters during the British Mandate of Palestine. A testament to their courage is documented in the Museum of Heroism within the fortress walls.

Girl in red watching the sea

Street view of Al-Jazzar Mosque >

With my driver pacing nearby, four Arab children approached and watched silently as I began painting this imposing mosque. Built in 1781 by Dahar el-Omar, a Bedouin sheik also known as Al-Jazzar (the "Butcher") for his cruelty, this majestic structure is considered the finest mosque in Israel.

Safed

PERCHED ON A HILL BENEATH THE MOUNTAINS OF MERON, northeast of the Sea of Galilee, is the legendary and mystical town of Safed. In the distant past, sages journeyed here to be near the tomb of Rabbi Shimon Bar Yochai, the revered 2nd-century sage who is believed to have written the foundations of the most mystical teachings in Judaism—the Cabala. As I wandered through the maze of narrow alleyways and cobblestone lanes, I felt as if I had stepped back in time. Above me, ancient stone archways and the domed rooftops of 16th-century houses loomed like guardians of the past. And the prayerful chants of devout men echoed through the streets from medieval synagogues. During the 16th century, when hundreds of thousands of Jews were forced to flee the Spanish Inquisition, some of them chose Safed as their new home. In 1563, the first Hebrew printing press in the Holy Land was established. Today, many renowned artists live in Safed. Drawn here by the simple and magical atmosphere of the area, their homes, studios and galleries, like the rest of the Old City, remain untouched by modern-day renovations. Their artwork reflects the mysterious spirit of the Cabala.

Stairway to the Synagogue

Black-clad men and colorfully dressed families wend their way through ancient stone archways and climb the many stairs to pray in medieval synagogues.

Safed
A CHRONOLOGY

Synagogue in Safed

Inside the turquoise blue Yosef Caro Synagogue a sign in Hebrew reads "Speaking is forbidden at times of prayer and the reading of the Torah."

PRE-CHRISTIAN ERA

After the deluge, Noah's son, Shem, and grandson, Ever, study the Torah in caves nearby.

538 BC—History of Safed goes back to the last days of the Second Temple, when fire signals were sent from its mountains to announce the New Moon and festivals.

CHRISTIAN ERA

AD 66–70—Priestly families settle here after the destruction of the Second Temple in Jerusalem. Jews of the Galilee build their citadel in Safed, under the direction of Josephus before his defection to the Romans, when he was sent north to prepare his brothers to revolt against Rome.

1050—Genizah documents attest to the existence of a Jewish community.

1140—Safed's history is obscure between Talmudic days and the Crusades. Safed reappears as "a fortress of great strength" between Akko and the Sea of Galilee, built by King Fulk of Anjou.

1168—Almaric I, King of Jerusalem, hands Safed over to the Knights Templar. On the summit of Mount Safed, the Crusaders build a castle to command the highway from Damascus, a Muslim entrenchment.

1122—Saladin conquers Safed.

1240—Safed is rebuilt by the Knights Templar.

1266—Safed passes from the Crusaders to the Mameluke Sultan Beibars, who continues to fortify it. Renaissance of Jewish life.

1481—Jewish community grows to 300 families, flourishing under the protection of Mameluke governors.

1492—Influx of refugees from Spain, when Spain expels its Jews.

1495—Jews of Safed trade spices, cheese, oil, and fruit.

1516—Ottoman conquest increases Jewish population. City becomes a center for Jewish mysticism (Cabala). Jews host Christian and Jewish pilgrims in their homes.

1563—The first Hebrew printing press is brought to the Holy Land by Eliezer Ashkenazi and his son, Isaac of Prague.

1500–1699—Golden Age of Safed dawns with the lore of the Cabala. Safed becomes the home of learned figures in Jewish history: Rabbi Isaac Luria (Ha'Ari), the greatest of the Cabalists, Yosef Caro, and Haim Vital. Turkish rule causes the city to deteriorate.

1742, 1769—A plague and an earthquake lead to the decline of Safed.

1778—300 Hassidim from Europe settle here.

1908—Improved Turkish administration brings the Jewish community to 8,000 and five years later to 11,000, in a population of 25,000.

1918—Safed is occupied by British forces.

1929—Arab nationalists kill Jews during riots.

1948—Israel's War of Independence. Number of Jews shrinks to 2,000. British evacuate town and permit Arab armies—comprised of Iraqi and Lebanese forces—to occupy two police buildings.

May 1948—The Hagannah's Palmach forces capture Safed, as the entire Arab population of some 10,000 flee.

To date—Merom, outside Safed, continues to be a focal point of pilgrims visiting the tombs of mystical Jews. Cabalist sages were buried here, and Safed's ancient synagogues and Talmudic scholars' burial places are also found here. Outstanding artist colony.

Exhibition hall and minaret

Some of the loveliest displays of Safed artists are exhibited in this large hall, where I purchased books of several local artists' works.

Cobbled street in Safed

Each of the doorways along the narrow cobblestone street opens to an art studio where the artist lives and displays his work.

Tiberias

RICH IN BIBLICAL HISTORY, THIS SPRAWLING CITY OF thirty thousand on the Sea of Galilee was established around AD 20 by the son of Herod the Great, Herod Antipater, who executed John the Baptist. It was here that Jesus gathered his disciples, preaching to the Jews, Greeks, and Romans in the crowded marketplaces. Having been built over a Jewish cemetery, the city was considered impure by devout Jews and Christians, who refused to live here for years. Eventually a ceremony of symbolic purification was performed by a rabbi, opening the way for settlement. By the middle of the 7th century Tiberias had grown into a prominent Christian center, second only to Jerusalem. But with the birth of the Arab conquest in AD 636, Tiberias was catapulted into an age of war, destruction, and natural disasters. Just beyond the city, the Horns of Hittim mark the spot where, in 1187, Saladin's Muslim forces crushed the Crusaders in a battle that leveled the city and ended their reign forever. Eventually resurrected, Tiberias stood until 1837, when a massive earthquake again reduced the city to rubble. The town was finally rebuilt by a small number of devout Jews, who lived in quiet harmony with their Arab neighbors until the War of Independence in 1948, when the Arabs fled. Today this capital city of the Galilee is the country's favorite winter resort and has become home to many of Israel's new Jewish immigrants.

Capernaum

Marking one of the most prominent Jewish and Christian sites of the Roman era, these remnants of a 2nd-century synagogue were built over ruins of the synagogue where Jesus preached and performed most of his miracles. The apostles Peter, Andrew, James, and John lived here during that time. The fish taken from the lake are called St. Peter's fish. They were delicious and were one of my favorite meals in Israel.

Tiberias

Capital of the Galilee. One of four holy cities.

A CHRONOLOGY

PRE-CHRISTIAN ERA

1250 BC—Settlement in Hammath Hot Springs, early site of Tiberias.

333–63 BC—Jewish fishermen inhabit area during Hellenistic times.

CHRISTIAN ERA

AD 20—Herod Antipater, son of Herod, builds Tiberias, naming it after the Roman Emperor Tiberius. The population is made up of landless people and freed slaves. Glass and pottery making, wool weaving, and fish ponds are the local industries.

70—Tiberias replaces Jerusalem as the center of Jewish learning, attracting great sages.

132—Rabbi Akiva supports Bar-Kochba's revolt against Rome and the struggle for Jewish freedom.

300–399—Site of superb early synagogue art: mosaics depicting the Ark of the Law and a candelabra.

614—Benjamin of Tiberias leads uprising against the Byzantines.

636—Arab rule. City becomes a center for tapestry.

700–799—The Jerusalem Talmud is compiled here and the vowel and punctuation system of the Hebrew script is devised by scholars.

1000–1127—Tiberias is capital of the Crusader principality of Galilee. The Crusaders build the walls of Tiberias.

1187—Crusader expedition to aid besieged Tiberias ends in disaster.

1190–1200—Rabbi Moses Ben Maimon, known as the Rambam—physician, philosopher, writer—was court doctor to Saladin in Cairo. Saladin's foe Richard the Lionheart sought unsuccessfully to persuade the Rambam to go to England with him.

1206—The Rambam, also known as Maimonides, is buried here.

1562—Turkish Sultan Suleiman I gives the city to Don Nasi to reestablish it as a Jewish city.

1600—Tiberias is in ruins.

1700—Sheik Zahir al-Amr, ruler of Galilee, rebuilds it.

1777—A group of Hassidim, who regard Tiberias as one of the four holy cities of the Land of Israel, rebuilds it again.

1833—Ibrahim Pasha restores the walls of Tiberias.

1837—A violent earthquake destroys most of the 16th-century wall and causes the deaths of some 1,000 Jews. Many flee to Jerusalem.

1912–1914—First Jewish Quarter is built outside the old Tiberias.

1920—The town of Kiryat Shmuel, named after British High Commissioner Sir Herbert Samuel, is established.

1922—Tiberias Hot Springs come into Jewish possession.

1948—The undeclared truce between some 6,000 Jews and Arabs is broken by an Arab attack, in anticipation of a Syrian invasion. The Hagannah counterattacks and the Arabs flee.

April 1948—The Golani Brigade, a company of the Palmach Third Battalion,

with forces of the Barak Battalion, force Arab gangs to flee or surrender. They liberate Tiberias.

1949—Transition camps for new immigrants are set up.

1960s—Camps disappear as newcomers settle around Kiryat Shmuel.

1991—A 1,900-year-old fishing village is uncovered near the Sea of Galilee.

1992—Tiberias prospers as a holiday resort on the Sea of Galilee.

< The Great Mosque

In the heart of the town of Tiberias is the Great Mosque, which was erected in the 18th century by Bedouin sheik Dahar el-Omar.

Tiberias Promenade

Galleries, shops, and outdoor cafes on this colorful promenade on the Sea of Galilee reminded me of Cannes on the French Riviera. Visitors arriving by boat ascend stairways anchored to the seawall.

The tomb of Rabbi Meir Ba'al Haness

Believed by some to be imbued with healing powers, this tomb on a Tiberian hillside contains the remains of Rabbi Meir Ba'al Haness, who became known as the Miracle Worker after he miraculously rescued his sister-in-law from the Romans. Called Meir—the Illuminator—because of his great teaching skills, the Rabbi's unselfish life was commemorated in 1873 by the building of a Sephardic synagogue. One year later an Ashkenazi synagogue was also constructed to mark his grave, where believers still come to pray for health and help with personal problems.

View of the Plaza Hotel, cafes, and
harbor from the Caesar Hotel

Sea of Galilee

The Romans called it Sea of Tiberias, meaning *jewel*. Its Hebrew name is Kinneret, meaning *harp*. The sea, which is really a lake, is harp-shaped. Fed by the Jordan River from the upper Galilee, the lake lies seven hundred feet below sea level, between Israel and Syria, and is surrounded by pearlish-brown mountains. Near the waters of the Sea of Galilee, where Jesus was said to have walked, the shoreline is dotted with churches marking the miracles Jesus reputedly performed, thus making the Galilee the "cradle of Christianity." It is also surrounded by some of the first kibbutzim—Jewish communal settlements that restored the land to food production.

The Church of the Beatitudes

Located on the Mountain of the Beatitudes, above the Sea of Galilee near Capernaum, this handsome octagonal structure occupies one of the holiest Christian sites in Israel. It was here that Jesus is said to have chosen his Twelve Apostles, and where he preached his Sermon on the Mount: "Blessed are the poor in spirit for theirs is the Kingdom of Heaven." Designed in 1936 by architect Antonio Barluzzi, each of the church's eight walls commemorates one of the Beatitudes, which means *blessings* in Latin. The seven virtues of man, referred to in the Sermon on the Mount, are beautifully symbolized on the church's intricate mosaic floor. Its rustic copper-domed chapel and the adjoining hospice are run today by Franciscan sisters. This historic locale offers a dazzling view of the Sea of Galilee.

Church of the Multiplication of Loaves and Fishes

This new church of the Multiplication, built in 1935 by the Order of the Benedictine Monks, marks the site in Tabga where Jesus is said to have performed his miracle of feeding thousands of followers with only a few loaves of bread and two fishes. The church is renowned for its exquisite multicolored mosaic floors preserved from the original ancient Byzantine church upon which it is built. Its inner court has one of the great views overlooking the Sea of Galilee.

Refreshments by the Sea of Galilee

Pink-domed church in Capernaum on the Sea of Galilee

Kibbutz Farod in the Galilee

Kibbutz is the Hebrew name for a collective settlement, a rural community based on mutual aid and social justice. The first kibbutzim were founded by young Zionists some forty years before the establishment of the State of Israel. They came to build a new way of life and to reclaim the soil of their ancient homeland. The kibbutzim in the Galilee are especially lovely, with many places to visit and to stay. Crossing the Sea of Galilee by boat to have lunch in Kibbutz Ein Gev was special. The day I was there, tourists—including over a hundred Japanese—were eating St. Peter's fish. Traveling through the Galilee, I was struck by the jewellike setting of Kibbutz Farod and had to paint it.

Nazareth

Viewed from a nearby hillside, this historic town, where Jesus spent much of his youth, seems to be frozen in time. Nestled amid rolling hills, the monumental Basilica of the Annunciation, which encompasses the remnants of earlier Byzantine churches dating from the 4th century, is the largest church in the Middle East. Completed in 1966, the church identifies the spot where the Archangel Gabriel is said to have appeared before the Virgin Mary, telling her that she has been chosen by God to bear his Son. In AD 326 the Emperor Constantine constructed the first church in Nazareth on the traditional site of Mary's home. Destroyed by invading Muslims in AD 636, Nazareth lay in ruins until it was restored by the Crusaders in the 12th century. A hundred years later, the Saracens completely devastated the city, which remained desolate for over 400 years until the 17th century, when a group of Franciscan monks returned to Nazareth and churches, monasteries, and schools were built. In recent times, thousands of pilgrims, seeking spiritual nourishment, have visited its shrines yearly. Modern-day Nazareth is the largest Arab city in Israel, with a population of over forty thousand Muslims and Arab-Christians.

About Dorothy Rice

Inside Jaffa Gate in Jerusalem

Ben Yehuda Street in Jerusalem

On the road to Jericho

WHEN DOROTHY RICE BEGAN PAINTING the locales and people of Israel, she embarked on the most exciting project of her career. She packed up her materials and walked the paths of history across Israel. Mingling with the people and recording her impressions, she captured the feeling and life of this multicultural country. Whenever a particular scene moved her emotionally, she set up her easel and painted on the spot, recording that moment in time. Though the people, locales, and architecture vary greatly, there is a subtle unity to her paintings.

Dorothy Rice studied at the Art Students League in New York City, the Otis/Parsons Art Institute, the Art Center College of Design in Los Angeles, and the University of Guadalajara, Mexico.

Her one-woman show of oils, "Serenata Mexicana," was such a runaway success at the prestigious Southwest Museum in Los Angeles that it was held over for two months. *Westways* magazine featured Dorothy Rice's lush Mexican paintings in an extensive illustrated article. And, honored in a country renowned for its great muralists, she is one of the few American artists ever invited to paint a mural in Mexico.

Dorothy Rice's oil, palate knife, and watercolor paintings are owned by many well-known collectors. Her work has been on exhibition in New York City; East Hampton; Tucson; in San Francisco at the Maxwell Gallery; in Los Angeles at the ARCO Center, Upstairs Gallery, Many Horses Gallery, and the Museum of Science and Industry; and recently in the Palm Springs Museum and the Eagle Art Gallery in Palm Desert. Currently, she is at work on a series of paintings of New York City.

Her book *Los Angeles with Love,* with a preface by Ray Bradbury, is a collector's item, a unique artist's vision of Los Angeles today. *Architectural Digest* devoted a major article to Dorothy Rice, which included many of her paintings.

As Ray Bradbury wrote: "Dorothy Rice has fresh eyes and her own palette. Which means a talent for making the familiar unfamiliar, younger than when you last saw it."